TEENAGER FOR NOW

Managing The Steps And Stages Of Teenage Life For Future Success

By Effell Williams, Sr.

Effell Williams Ministries Publishing
Selma, Alabama

Published by Effell Williams Ministries of Selma
PO Box 969
Selma, Alabama 36702

Cover Design by Justin Foster jus10foster.com
Title Page Image by Candace Pope

ISBN 978-0-9970914-2-7

Printed in the United States of America

For more information and other products
www.effellwilliams.org

CONTENTS

Teenager for Now

Introduction

Teenager for Now

By definition, a teenager can be described as a person between the ages of 13-19. Another name that could be used to describe this period in one's life is adolescence, which is a period of physical and social growth from childhood to adult. What does it mean to you to be a teenager? What do you think will be or is required of you during these formative years? How will you manage what is expected of you? These are probably your most important years, for they will prepare you for becoming a mature adult. Keep in mind that your parents have been teenagers also, and they are well aware of the many pitfalls that will confront you during this time in your life. Take your time; don't rush through these important years; ask questions; seek guidance, and learn all that you can during this period of your life, for you will benefit greatly in your later years.

You are becoming an adult. You are not a child anymore, but you are not a mature adult either. You are right in the middle at the place designed to prepare you for adulthood, and then on to fatherhood or motherhood. You are in the stage of your life that is known as your formative years. Everything you hear, see, and say will help to shape who you are, what you believe, and how you will behave. It can be your most misunderstood period of your life, due in part to your quest for your own identity and your attempt to break free of the control that you think others have over you, including – in some cases – your parents. Your later adult life will be shaped in large part by what you learned, how you were taught, and how you developed during your teenage years.

Again, another name that can be used for the teenage years is adolescence, which can be defined into three stages: early adolescence (around ages 10-14), middle adolescence (around ages 15-17), and late adolescence (around ages 18-21). This book is centered mainly with ages 13-19 and is an attempt to assist you in developing into the mature adult necessary for you to have a successful life. The more information you are given, the easier it will be for you to make sound decisions. Remember also that all of your teachers, leaders, and parents have been teenagers before; and they are committed to assisting you during these formative years in an effort to see that you achieve your maximum potential. Your relationships, home training, associations, and behavior will all work in concert to develop who you are and what you will become. Take your time, follow instructions, be obedient, and be respectful to assure that you develop a solid foundation necessary for you to be a successful adult.

Take your time growing up, maturing, and learning all that you can during this period. You will reach adulthood soon enough. Don't allow the temptations to get you to speed up the process, thereby bypassing necessary steps that you need to take now. Don't worry, these years are the perfect time for you to seek advice from your parents, ministers, teachers, and other leaders on what is necessary for you to successfully navigate your teenage years. Be open to corrections: they are necessary for your continued maturity.

Enjoy the freedom of these years; don't try to be an adult just yet. Trust the process; you will get there soon enough. Be obedient to your parents, stay in a real relationship with your God, study to be the best student that you can be, be careful who you allow in your inner circle, and keep a positive self-image and mindset, for it will all pay off in the end.

Teenager for Now

Chapter 1
How Does it All Work?

Teenager for Now

As a teenager, you are at the most exciting time of your life. You are learning new things about life itself, meeting all kinds of people, learning more about being a young man or young lady, learning more about Christ, and trying to figure out what you want to do with your life. You find so many things to get involved in and hope that they are real. You want more space from your parents because they simply don't seem to understand what you are going through. You find it hard sometimes to trust people because you have been hurt before. With all these things going on in your mind, you wonder if anyone else has gone through what you are facing and dealing with. The answer is yes! You are not alone. It is called growing up.

You have been waiting on your teenage years; well, now they are here. You may feel as if you are already prepared to be treated as an adult. However, don't rush yourself, for the learning process has just begun. You will be given more responsibilities around the house, ones that now you will be expected to take care of without being asked to do. This is the time you should ask lots of questions, even if they seem silly to others. During this learning process, there are no bad questions. So many things will be much better for you as a teenager by having as much information as you can obtain before trying something that you have never done. Yes, be excited about your teenage years, but don't rush them away. This stage of your life is critical in your overall development. The right crowd, the right environment, the right education, the right mindset, the right attitude, and the right plans will all play a major role in your future adult life. There will be pressure to grow up faster than you would like or are ready to do. Don't get in a hurry. Trust your parents, older siblings (if you have any), your church, and others for godly advice during this stage of your life. There will be many temptations to do and try things now that were not offered to you before. Never forget what you have been taught. Look at these things this way: if they were not good for you before, they are not good for you now! You now being a teenager does not make a forbidden act appropriate or right now that you are one.

You have the awesome blessing of your parents who have been through many of the things that you will now be faced with. Always remember that your parents did not become adults over night; they were teenagers also. It may not seem like it, but they were teenagers at one time. Trust them to do what they believe is best and right for you. These years present a time when you will begin to question why you can't go here or there, do this or that, have that, or be this or that. The pull of your peers and friends will be great upon you to rebel against what you know to be right. There is something about your teenage years that will make you question why you must wait to experience some of the things that you will be tempted to do. That's why parents are here; they are empowered and ordained by God to lead you through these formative years called teenage hood.

You may feel that parents sometimes don't seem to understand what you are facing. However, they love you and only want what is best for you in all things that concern you. Don't ever allow anyone at any time to make you doubt the care and love your parents have for you. If you feel that your parents don't show you the love that you think they should, talk with them, not others, about this. Never share your problems or feelings with other teens who have no relationship with their own parents. This is very dangerous; therefore, avoid it at all cost. Parents are not perfect; however, they have the awesome responsibility of making sure that these teenage years are positive, beneficial, and enjoyable for you. Yes, your parents may seem to forget that they were once teenagers; however, that is not the case. Because they do know what it is like to be a teenager, they will make certain decisions concerning you at this time. You take your time maturing; you will, God willing, be an adult much longer than you will be a teenager. Allow your parents to help you walk through this process for your benefit. You have it pretty good at the moment: no rent, no bills, no car payments, and no grocery bills. Don't allow peer pressure to make you mess this up. Ease into this process, allowing your parents and older siblings to assist you in navigating these formative years. You will notice that the desire for more freedom will increase at each of your teenage years. However, know that all behavior is learned, and if you remember what you have been taught from your family and others, the temptation to go against your training will not overwhelm you.

Yes, you are a teenager for now; what does that mean in terms of your relationship with your parents, siblings, and others in authority? It means new opportunity for more freedom, the desire to wear what you want, look like you want to, go where you want to go, but not yet having the power to do so. Keep in mind that you are a teenager, not a mature person at this time. Try with all of your might to grow gracefully into the mature person that God would have you to become. Listen, be kind, keep good manners, follow teaching, obey your parents, watch your words, and enjoy being a teenager. It's the time of your life where you can have all the fun you can tolerate and not have to worry about adult responsibilities. Keep yourself in touch with your home life, school, church, and other organizations that have been put here to help you. Never knowingly act in disrespect or in disobedience to your home training and teaching of your house of faith. God has promised you a long and good life (Ephesians 6:1-3) if you honor your parents, and nothing shows more honor to them than for you to walk in obedience to them and your God. Long and good life – that's what God has promised you. No matter how much your friends may try to get you to go against what you have been taught and what you have learned from your parents, reject it at every turn. Remember, a temporary act can bring a lifetime of problems and struggles later in life; you have been given a path that your parents, along with God, can lead you to adulthood and propel you to a successful life. What you will face in your teenage hood is something that your parents or guardians have experienced themselves. Don't be afraid to ask questions about anything that concerns your daily issues. Never try to go into it alone; use the resources that God has made available to you. There is no such thing as a bad question, so never be afraid to ask if you do not know what to do next.

Each year, you will become more of what you will eventually become as an adult. Take your time, learn from your parents, and reject any information from your peers or friends that is oppose to the teaching that you know to be true. Enjoy being a teenager for now; these are developmental years, and they will set you on a course that will direct the rest of your life.

Chapter 2
What About the
Boyfriend/Girlfriend Thing?

As a teenager, one of the most common experiences that you will face or be confronted with is or will be the boyfriend/girlfriend experience. When do I have one? Should I have one? Who should he/she be? Is it ok with God to have one? You should not try to answer any of the aforementioned questions without the aid and advice of your parents. It is their training and influence that should drive you in all of these questions. You will be pulled into many directions; however, leaning on and trusting in the advice and guidance of your parents and spiritual leader can assist you greatly in this matter. Having a boyfriend or girlfriend should be far down the line of important things for you to be concerned about at the moment. The model for you to consider following includes getting a quality education (nothing will prepare you for success in life as a good education can) and developing a solid Christian foundation (Remember now thy creator in the days of thy youth, while the evil day come not, nor the years

draw nigh, when thou shalt say, I have no pleasure in them…
Ecclesiastes 12:1). Enjoy being a teenager, and lean on the
advice and teaching of your parents and others so that you can
learn the secret of success from them. Then, and only then,
if there is still time available, should you worry about the
boyfriend/girlfriend thing. Enjoy being young because it will
not happen again.

Be careful who you make your friends. Remember, behavior is learned. You will pick up the behavior of the people
with whom you associate. Also, you will become a product
of your environment. The Bible states: "Evil communication
corrupts good manners." All behavior, good or bad, grows
out of associations. Never allow yourself to be pressured into
doing something that you know is against what you believe,
what you have been taught, and what you know is wrong. If
others call you "old fashioned" because of your belief, take it
as a compliment. Drug abuse and promiscuous behavior can

never be an escape for you. Stand your ground and remember your teaching and training – you will be much better off. To the best of your abilities, try using sports, hobbies, church functions, and extracurricular activities to fulfill your social needs during this period.

Friends are a valuable asset in your personal development. Friends can help or harm your growth through your teenage years. Know that there are friends and then there are associates. Friends will make you better, expecting nothing in return. On the other hand, those who are associates or acquaintances more often than not will seek something for nothing from you. Real friends will complement what you have been taught and will not seek to lead you away from it. The Bible declared: "Two cannot walk together unless they be agreed." Do all you can to befriend only those whom you trust to have your best interest, those who have proven that they can be trusted, and only those who will not walk away when you have disagreements. Who you befriend can affect every area of your life. The ones who are true friends will make your time as a teenager enjoyable, not stressful. To the best of your ability, make sure that you are not pushed or deceived into befriending someone who will cause you to stop growing academically, socially, and spiritually. A lacking in either of these areas will be harmful to your continued growth. Never feel bad about being picky in choosing who you allow as a friend. Your friends will be either good or bad for your current and future success. Remember, in order to develop any kind of relationship, one must agree with the person he/she will be involved with. This includes agreeing to what will and will not be acceptable, what will be the basis of the relationship, and the character of the relationship. Your current situation will either be improved or damaged by those with whom you surround yourself.

Do your very best to learn what is the most important

thing in life as a teenager, for in doing so you will have a better understanding where to place this boyfriend/girlfriend thing. You have so much to be engaged with: school, extra-curricular activities, family responsibilities, and your relationship with your Lord God. Yes, there will be time for that special person, if you will; however, take your time, develop in every area that is required for maturity. Talk with someone whom you know has your best interest at heart for meaningful advice on the boyfriend/girlfriend subject matter.

Chapter 3
Music and My Development

No music (sound) is sinful or wrong by itself. However, it is the words of the song that make the secular music harmful or ungodly. If you will take a serious listen to what the words are saying, you will find it pretty difficult to justify some of the songs that you hear on a daily basis. Music should reflect your character and represent who you are and what you really believe in as a Christian. This is one area that the Devil will use to trap you, distract you, and mislead you as a teenager. The best way to determine what you should or should not be listening to is to ask yourself, "Does this music enhance my character or harm my character?" Know for sure that what you continuously hear will eventually get into your heart and mind. Therefore, it is very important what you allow to be played in your presence. The words of the song gets into your soul and can cause you to act out some of what is said. Remember, "As a man thinketh, so is he." Always be in charge of what you listen to when it comes to the kind of music you will tolerate.

Music has been described as the universal language of the world. It can calm you, lift you, inspire you, and cause you to do what you would not ordinarily do. As stated before, music is neither good nor bad; it is the words that cause a particular song to be appropriate or not. It is your responsibility to know and understand what you accept as your music of choice. Never allow music to define you, but if you do, let it be according to your character. Music has long been used in all kinds of settings and has encouraged people to seek things beyond what they currently possessed. The music should lift you, encourage you, enhance you culturally, and cause you to feel better after listening to it. If the music lyrics degrade, offend, mock, or belittle others, should you really be listening to it? Know for a certainty that what you continuously hear will eventually get into your heart, which will then come out of your mouth. You will rehearse what you hear, and it will become part of your regular vocabulary and daily communication. Be reminded that music is not the issue, but it is the words of the song that will have an impact upon you. If you are not comfortable with the music that you are hearing, don't compromise your beliefs. There is a message behind every song, and every message is not a positive one. Please take note of the fact that the enemy would love to have a negative influence upon you through the avenue of your music. Keep a sound mind when it comes to what you choose to listen to in music, for it can set you upon a path that will affect your behavior, actions, beliefs, and your relationship with family and friends. Know that if the music is disrespectful, it can cause you to begin to lean in that direction. The lyrics, lyrics, lyrics: this is what makes the songs influential concerning you and your behavior. Think of it this way: would your mom, sister, or dad be offended in the songs that you are listening to? If they would, do you think that you should be listening to it? Let this be a measuring stick for you accepting what kind of music will occupy your music library.

Teenager for Now

Chapter 4
Church Life vs Social Life

God calls the young to be examples also. It is not the intent of the Lord for you to be denied a full teenage life. However, always remember that you are a believer at all times, regardless of the position or situation. Never think of attending church or living a Christian life as boring or not interesting. You already know how to have fun; however, the fun must always be in line with what you know to be right. Your social life does not have to compete with your church responsibilities. Church attendance is not an option; therefore, you should not think of it as a hit or miss proposition. We attend church to worship our Lord and to gain wisdom and insight to help us face and handle the problems and challenges that we will face on a regular basis. Never attend church for anyone else. Worship God for yourself, not for others. What knowledge you obtain now will be with you for a life time. See the church as a refueling station, and never leave it without being filled with something for the next day. The church, along with your family, is where you learn good and sound Christian values, which are to be incorporated in your everyday life. In the church, you learn one of the most important messages that you can learn about guaranteed success in the Word of God: "Trust in the Lord with all of thine heart; and lean not unto thine own understanding. In all thy ways acknowledge Him, and He shall direct thy path" (Proverb 3:5-6). This is God's promise to you, and it will never fail.

You are told in scripture: "Don't let the excitement of youth cause you to forget your Creator. Honor Him in your youth before you grow old and say life is not pleasing anymore. Remember Him before the light of the sun, moon, and stars is dim to your old eyes, and rain clouds continually darken your sky. Yes, remember your Creator now while you are young before the silver cord of life snaps and the golden bowl is broken" (Ecclesiastes 12:1-2,6). Your relationship with your Lord and Savior is vital to your success now and in the future. He loves you unconditionally and longs for a relation-ship with you. Don't wait until you get older to develop a meaningful relationship with Him; make it happen now. You will be glad that you did. Friends and peers that pull you away from or weaken your relationship with God and your church attendance should be avoided whenever possible.

Yes, you should embrace a good, clean, and positive social life; however, this should not interfere with your church life. Every adult has been a teenager like you, and they are in no way against you having fun and enjoying your teenage years. However, having gone through the teenage years themselves, parents are mindful of the importance of having a good spiri-tual relationship with the Lord. What you have been taught or are currently being taught is done to help you move through these formative years with as much success as possible. To the best of your ability, put God first, then your family, your ed-ucation, peer relationships, and then extracurricular activities.

Chapter 5
Stages of Teenage Development

Every state of your development is very important because it prepares you for the next one you must encounter. As a teenager, there are three important areas that you must develop before entering adulthood. Failure to properly develop in these areas can and probably will cause problems in your later adult life. This is why it is critical that you get proper guidance, information, and directions as a teenager so that you can properly prepare for the good life God has prepared for you. The first area that you must develop is a positive self-image or positive self-worth of who you are. Nothing worse will keep you from fulfilling your dreams as a negative self-image or self-worth of who you are. No one can make you feel good about yourself if you do not have a positive image of yourself. No matter what has happened to you in the past, you can and must think positively about who you are and what you can accomplish. The scripture declares: "For as he thinketh in his heart, so is he"; therefore, you are what you think you are. If you think you can or think you can't, you are right in both cases. You must keep a positive outlook on your teenage life and not allow negative peers or influences to make you feel bad about who you are. No matter where you were born, where you live, or who your parents are; you are special and can achieve what you set your mind to do. Never allow negative thoughts or words to make you feel bad about things around you or who you are. Learn as a teenager how to speak positive words over your current situation, your dreams, and where you want to go in life. According to the Bible: "Death and life are in the power of the tongue"; therefore, you must be careful how you speak because your words can cause things around you to either prosper or not. What you say and think now as a teenager can help develop your thinking and communication skills that are so necessary for a positive adult life.

You must always keep in mind that God has made you to be awesome. In fact, the Bible states: "You are fearfully and wonderfully made." A positive mindset about yourself is crucial to becoming all that God has purposed you to be. Remember, you will become what you continually think. Don't allow thoughts that are negative to live in your mind or heart. You do not have to compare yourself to anyone else; in fact, the Devil will constantly try to get you to compare yourself to others in an effort to get you to feel negatively about who you are as compared to someone else. When the thought shows up tempting you to feel bad about who you are, just remember that you have everything that you need to be successful in your current stage of development. God did not make you like anyone else, but He made you to be just the way you are.

Always be mindful that you have promises from God for a good and long life if you honor your parents, and it is His will for you to succeed in life. Conquering self-doubt, negative self-image, and uncertainties of your abilities is a must for you to become all that God has planned for you to be. You can never achieve what you don't believe that you can achieve. Whatever makes you feel bad about yourself must be identified, addressed, and adjusted so that you can overcome and conquer whatever it may be. You are the apple of God's eye, regardless of what others may think of you. You can do, according to scripture, "all things through Christ which strengthens you." Remember, you were created in the image and likeness of God, so you can be sure that you are in good company. Your teenage years can be a tough time when it comes to managing and cultivating a positive self-image. You can experience peer pressure to look a certain way, act a certain way, and even talk a certain way, all just so that you can fit in. However, through all of this, always, always remember who you are, whose you are, and what you represent. Don't ever allow peer pressure to make you feel bad about who and what you are. You are loved, appreciated, and needed by your family and real friends. Know for a fact that what you do or do not have does not make you who you are. You are more than things, places, positions, or looks. With all of your might, cast down negative thoughts or imaginations as quickly as possible before they can cause you to become depressed or unhappy about yourself. Nothing can be more destructive as a negative mindset or negative self-image. Embrace who God has created you to be and what your family has helped you to achieve. You are not required to please those who have no stake in your future. Work hard to develop and keep a positive self-image; it will certainly pay off in later in your teenage years and adulthood.

The second area that you must develop as a teenager is the ability to form positive associations/friends. With whom you keep company or make friends will determine where you are headed in life. Your friends will either influence you, or you will influence them. According to the Bible, "Two cannot walk together, except they be agreed." In other words, you and your friends must agree to a certain behavior or lifestyle together before forming a friendship. You must develop your standards and not lower them in order to be friends with anyone. Those with whom you associate will help determine how you speak, dress, believe, act, think, or carry yourself. Therefore, it is very important that you think long and hard before forming a relationship with anyone. Never make friends to be seen, heard, accepted, or recognized. Everything reproduces after its own kind. You will be a product of your environment. The friends or associations that you develop as a teenager can affect you even into your adulthood. Be careful not to make friends with those who will make your good name become a bad one. Friends really can make or break you in terms of your reputation. Your life as a teenager should be one of fun, happiness, development, and enjoyment. Learn now when and to whom to say no. As mentioned before, never lower your standards to make friends or associations with anyone. Your friends don't have to believe exactly like you; however, they must possess similar behavior, character, and lifestyle that complement yours. Please keep in mind that you will either change them or they will change you. If someone is going to change you, let it be in a positive manner. Behavior is learned; therefore, don't learn from the wrong teachers.

You should always remember that you will become a product of your surroundings. You will form ideas, opinions, and values based upon what you are constantly hearing or being around. Everything reproduces after its own kind, and you will be no exception. You cannot be a part of one thing and become another. The Bible gives excellent instructions on associations. It states: "Oh, the joys of those who do not follow the advice of the wicked, or stand around with sinners, or join in with mockers. But they delight in the Law of the Lord, meditating on it day and night" (Psalm 1:1-2). This simply means you cannot follow wrong advice or people and end up in the right place. Your associations will go a long way in where you will end up in life. Know that you will pick up the habits of those with whom you continue to associate. Make who you befriend and associate with a top priority in your development. Ask questions, seek godly guidance, and never go against your godly training and teaching. Know that evil or bad communication will corrupt good manners. Everything that you are constantly around will affect you in some way, good or bad. No matter how mature you think you may be, you will be influenced by your associations and relationships. No matter how much you have been taught by your parents and church, it will be challenged by what you constantly hear and see. Your character is formed by what you see, hear, and say. It is through these that information and thoughts enter your mind and heart. Peer pressure can only be applied on you when what you have been taught is confronted by what is in opposition to it. Know those with whom you associate, trusting what you have been taught versus what may be popular at the moment. There is a big difference between the two.

The third area that you must develop as a teenager is a good name or reputation. The Bible states in Proverbs 22:1: "A good name is rather to be chosen than great riches." Also, the Book of Ecclesiastes declares: "A good name is better than precious ointment." Your reputation is what others think of you, be it good or bad. No one can give you a good reputation; your good name or reputation must be earned. You earn it based upon what you do or not do, what you say, where you go, with whom you associate, and how well you interact with and treat others. A reputation is like money: the amount you have determines what you can purchase. Your good name must be guarded with all your might. It is gold and silver in life that you can purchase without being rich or famous. Don't allow anyone to damage your good name for any reason, if at all possible. Please remember that your reputation will follow you wherever you go. In fact, your name will get to a place even before you actually arrive there in person. Learn to do good at all times, and you will find others who will help you succeed in life. Be very weary of those who would attempt to hurt or destroy your good name. Your life, your family, your job, your success in school, dating, and most of all your future will be shaped by your reputation. If you do not have the kind of reputation that you know you should have, change your behavior and/or associations. The kind of life that you will experience at all levels will depend upon it. You will have a much smoother transition from teenage hood to adulthood if you develop yourself in the above-mentioned areas.

As mentioned earlier, a reputation is the belief or opinion

that is generally held about someone or something. In other words, your reputation is what others think of you, good or bad. Your name or reputation is your character, and it is like wealth for you. Without it, you are not able to purchase anything. Guard your good name/reputation at all cost. It's hard to build a good one, but it is very easy to lose. The Bible states: "Let not your good be evil spoken of," meaning don't allow something good be done in a manner to bring dishonor to what is good.

You can be sure that the Devil will try with all of his powers to destroy or damage your name or reputation. Therefore, it is critical that you try to avoid anything or anyone that would bring damage to them. The Bible lets us know that the "thief only comes to steal, to kill, and to destroy." Don't help him in any way to destroy what you have built up. Your reputation was earned by behavior, and that's the only way it can be lost. Guard your words, actions, and behavior, for they will continue to build or destroy your name. You don't have time to spend in your later years trying to repair your name or reputation from what you were in your teenage years. Remember, true or not, your reputation is a belief or opinion that others think about you. You will be treated and respected for your name. No matter how unfair this may seem, this is how you will have to go through life – on what others think about you. Do all you can to help keep your name good among others around you. Be diligent to build a name/reputation that you, your family, and your friends can all be proud of and always willing to recommend you to anyone else. Failure to do so can cause years of struggling, hardship, and disappointments. Know that your gift and skills can take you where your character cannot keep you. In other words, you are only as good as your name and reputation will allow you to be. YOU ARE A TEENAGER FOR NOW; LEARN, DEVELOP, ENJOY, AND GROW, for you can never regain these years again. Blessings.

Teenager for Now

Chapter 6
Helpful Hints

1. Submit daily to the Word of God:
   A. Try to read at least one chapter in the Word each day. Read about the promises of God to you.
   B. Commit to learning one scripture verse each week.
2. Develop a meaningful prayer life:
   A. Make it a practice to pray each day, morning and evening at least.
   B. Pray the Word of God.
   C. Be open and honest with God during your prayer time.
3. Attend church regularly:
   A. Church attendance is not an option. The Bible states: "Forsake not the assembling together of yourselves."
   B. Make it a priority. Make every effort not to get distracted when it's church time.
   C. Good church attendance will assist greatly in your spiritual development.
4. Get involved in youth activities at your church:
   A. Teaching is critical for your spiritual walk with God.
   B. Fellowship with other youth in your church.

C. Ask questions that you may be having problems
with.

5.   Make Christ and the Kingdom top priority in your
life:

A. Putting God first will allow you to experience
God's presence in your life.

B. You are told to seek the Kingdom of God first, and
all essential things will be given unto you.

C. In all of your ways, acknowledge the Lord, and He
will direct your path.

6. Share your faith:

A. Be a witness for Christ every chance you get.

B. Be an example to believers and non-believers.

C. The more you share your faith with other youth,
the more God will give you reasons to share it.

7. Testify of God goodness to you as often as you can:

A. Scripture declares: "They overcame him [the drag-
on] by the Blood of the Lamb, and by the word of
their testimony." Testifying increases your faith.

B. Some need to know what God has done/is doing
for you so that they can be encouraged.

C. If He did it for you, He can do it for others as well.

SOME IMPORTANT THINGS TO CONSIDER DURING THIS TIME

1. FAMILY VALUES:
   A. Never forget your family training. Things will come and go, but your home training will go with you wherever you go.
   B. They are the foundation for your life, now and in the future.
   C. Seek to build upon them, and reject all things that would destroy them.

2. SPIRITUAL RELATIONSHIP:
   A. The promises of God are locked up in your personal relationship with Him. Grow your faith on a regular basis.
   B. Salvation is not optional.
   C. Regular church attendance is a must for spiritual development.

3. EDUCATION:
   A. Next to your relationship with your family and your God, nothing is as important as a good education.
   B. You will struggle in life without one.

STEPS TO SALVATION

Romans 10:9-10: "That if thou shalt confess with thy mouth the Lord Jesus, and shalt believe in thine heart that God hath raised Him from the dead, thou shalt be saved. For with the heart man believeth unto righteousness; and with the mouth confession is made unto salvation."

1. ADMIT
   A. Admit that you were born into sin; therefore, you are in need of a Savior.
2. BELIEVE
   A. Believe that Jesus died and rose from the dead to save you from your sins.
3. CONFESS
   A. Confess with your mouth that you accept Jesus Christ as your Lord and savior, for it is with your mouth that you acknowledge Him as Savior.
4. BE BAPTIZED
   A. He that believeth and is baptized shall be saved. To be baptized is to show the world that you have been buried and resurrected with Christ.
5. JOIN A GOOD BIBLE BELIEVING AND TEACHING CHURCH

    C. God said "My people are destroyed for the lack of knowledge"; this could be both spiritual and natural. Don't settle for anything less than a good education.

4. FRIENDS/ASSOCIATIONS:

    A. They can make you better or worse, depending upon who you befriend.

    B. Two cannot walk together unless they be in agreement.

    C. Pray before befriending anyone; moving too quickly can be detrimental.

5. GOOD NAME/REPUTATION:

    A. This is your wealth that money cannot buy. It will determine how others treat you, help you, and receive you. Guard your good name with all your might.

    B. Avoid all that will be harmful to your good name.

    C. It can do more than even your skills can do.

6. PERSONAL GROWTH:

    A. The more you grow in your life, the more you will experience the many benefits life has to offer.

    B. The growth should be both spiritual and personal. If you remain the same, nothing will ever change or improve.

    C. Seek godly counsel from parents, ministers,

and other leaders on what is required for personal growth.

7. FUTURE PLANS:

  A. Always plan for what you want to achieve. Failure to plan may be a plan to fail.

  B. In all of your ways acknowledge God, and He has promised to direct your path.

  C. Plan with God in mind, and He will include you in His.

ABOUT THE AUTHOR

Bishop Effell Williams is the founding pastor of Tabernacle of Praise Churches, Inc. with locations in Selma, Uniontown, Birmingham, and Decatur, Alabama. He is also the Presiding Bishop of the AL/MS Fellowship of churches with fellowship churches in Alabama and Mississippi.

He is a member of the Global United Fellowship under the leadership of Bishop Neil C. Ellis, of Nassau, Bahamas. Bishop Williams serves as Provincial Bishop of the South Central Region for the Global Fellowship.

Bishop Williams is a retired educator and holds a B.S. and Master's degree in Business Administration and Counseling from the University of West Alabama in Livingston, Alabama. He holds a B.S. and Master's degree in Theology from Christian Life School of Theology in Columbus, Georgia.

He is married to the former Brenda Faye Smith of Lisman, Alabama, and has three children: Alesha Jackson, Andrea Pope, and Effell, Jr. He has one granddaughter, Ambrielle, and two sons-in-law, Apostle Wade Jackson and Jarrod Pope.

You can follow Bishop Williams on Facebook and Instagram. Email address: www.effellw@icloud.com or www.pastor@topchurch.org. Mailing address: Bishop Effell Williams, P.O. Box 969, Selma, AL 36702.